KOREANS IN AMERICA

web enhanced at www.inamericabooks.com

STACY TAUS-BOLSTAD

LERNER PUBLICATIONS COMPANY / MINNEAPOLIS

Current information and statistics quickly become out of date. That's why we developed **www.inamericabooks.com**, a companion website to the **In America** series. The site offers lots of additional information—downloadable photos and maps and up-to-date facts through links to additional websites. Each link has been carefully selected by researchers at Lerner Publishing Group and is regularly reviewed and updated. However, Lerner Publishing Group is not responsible for the accuracy or suitability of material on websites that are not maintained directly by us. It is recommended that students using the Internet be supervised by a parent, a librarian, a teacher, or another adult.

Note to Readers: This book uses the Revised Romanization of Korean for Korean proper nouns. Please see page 8 for more information.

Copyright © 2005 by Lerner Publications Company

Lerner Publications Company
A division of Lerner Publishing Group
241 First Avenue North
Minneapolis, MN 55401 U.S.A.

Website address: www.lernerbooks.com

Library of Congress Cataloging-in-Publication Data

Taus-Bolstad, Stacy.
    Koreans in America / by Stacy Taus-Bolstad.
        p.   cm. — (In America)
    Includes bibliographical references and index.
    ISBN: 0–8225–4874–7 (lib. bdg. : alk. paper)
    1. Korean Americans—History—Juvenile literature. 2. Immigrants—United States—History—Juvenile literature. 3. Korean Americans—Juvenile literature. I. Title. II. Series: In America (Minneapolis, Minn.)
    E184.K6T38 2005
    973'.04957–dc22   2004017726

Manufactured in the United States of America
1 2 3 4 5 6 – JR – 10 09 08 07 06 05

CONTENTS

INTRODUCTION

In America, a walk down a city street can seem like a walk through many lands. Grocery stores sell international foods. Shops offer products from around the world. People strolling past may speak foreign languages. This unique blend of cultures is the result of America's history as a nation of immigrants.

Native peoples have lived in North America for centuries. The next settlers were the Vikings. In about A.D. 1000, they sailed from Scandinavia to lands that would become Canada, Greenland, and Iceland. In 1492 the Italian navigator Christopher Columbus landed in the Americas, and more European explorers arrived during the 1500s. In the 1600s, British settlers formed colonies that, after the Revolutionary War (1775–1783), would become the United States. And in the mid-1800s, a great wave of immigration brought millions of new arrivals to the young country.

Immigrants have many different reasons for leaving home. They may leave to escape poverty, war, or harsh governments. They may want better living conditions for themselves and their children. Throughout its history, America has been known as a nation that offers many opportunities. For this reason, many immigrants come to America.

Moving to a new country is not easy. It can mean making a long, difficult journey. It means leaving home and starting over in an unfamiliar place. But it also means using skill, talent, and determination to build a new life. The In America series tells the story of immigration to the United States and the search for fresh beginnings in a new country—in America.

KOREANS IN AMERICA

Koreans began moving to the United States in small numbers during the late 1800s. But large numbers of Korean immigrants didn't start arriving in the United States until 1903. After that, three distinct waves of Korean immigration took place. The first was from 1903 to 1924, when a poor economy forced Korean farmers and laborers to seek work outside their homeland. The second wave of immigration happened at the end of the Korean War (1950–1953). Korean spouses of U.S. soldiers and Korean children adopted by American families were allowed to move into the United States to join their new families.

The third and largest wave of immigration started in 1965, in response to less restrictive immigration laws. Until then Koreans had made up a small minority population in America, numbering only around 10,000. After the immigration laws changed, nearly 800,000 Koreans moved to the United States. By the early twenty-first century, Korean Americans had grown to a population of more than one million, becoming the fourth largest Asian group in America. The biggest populations of Korean Americans live in California, New York, and Washington.

The history of Korean immigration is fairly short compared to that of most ethnic groups who came to America from Europe and Asia, and the number of Americans of Korean ancestry is still relatively small. Yet, in that short history, Korean Americans have done very well in their adopted country. As their numbers grow, Korean Americans are becoming a more visible part of the American population. They continue to make a place for themselves in American politics, business, and the arts.

1 LIFE IN KOREA

The Korea Peninsula lies in East Asia. The peninsula, an area of land almost completely surrounded by water, is bordered by the Yellow Sea (also called Hwang Sea or Hwanghae by Koreans) to the west and the Sea of Japan (called East Sea in Korea) to the east. The island nation of Japan lies to the south and east. China and Russia lie to the north.

The Korea Peninsula stretches about 600 miles north to south and about 185 miles east to west, and it occupies 85,774 square miles. The southern part of the peninsula juts out into the Korea Strait, which connects the Yellow Sea to the Sea of Japan. China and Russia make up the Korea Peninsula's neighbors to the north, the only area not surrounded by water. About three thousand islands belong to Korea, with most of these in the Yellow Sea. Since World War II (1939–1945), the peninsula has been divided into two nations—North Korea and

South Korea. A 2.5–mile–wide strip of land, called the Demilitarized Zone (DMZ), separates these two countries.

The Korea Peninsula's geography ranges from mountainous and rugged in the North and along the eastern coast to low–lying coastal plains in the southern and western regions. These geographic differences result in a varied climate. The northern part of the peninsula experiences a definite change of seasons, with cold winters and warm summers. In the South, the climate is warmer and more humid all year long. The peninsula has a wide range of plant life, including the bright flowers of the South and the sturdier trees of the North.

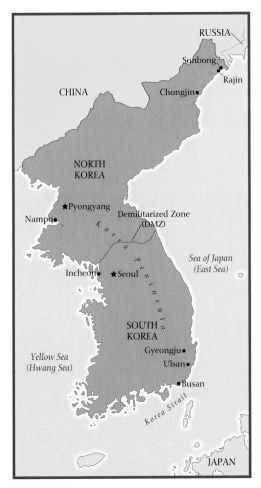

This map of the Korea Peninsula in modern times and other maps can be downloaded at www.inamericabooks.com.

EARLY CIVILIZATIONS

The Korean people have a long and proud history. Archaeological evidence shows that humans started living on the Korea Peninsula sometime around 700,000 B.C. Little is known about these early inhabitants, but historians believe that they hunted large mammals and gathered wild plants for food. They lived a nomadic life, moving from place to place with each season to follow the animal herds that they hunted. They also began fishing along the coasts and rivers.

Artifacts show that humans developed a more settled way of life around 4000 B.C. People living on the peninsula began growing their own food and raising livestock. They stopped moving with the seasons and built more permanent homes. They created pottery from clay and fashioned tools from stone and animal bones. Over the centuries, people worked with metals and soon developed more complex tools and weapons. They also began trading with other groups, including the Chinese. This contact with outside influences would have an important effect on the development of the modern Korean nations.

KNOW YOUR ABCS

Because Korean is written using symbols other than the letters that the Roman alphabet uses in English, Korean words are Romanized (transferred into the Roman alphabet) for English speakers. The two main ways to Romanize Korean are the McCune-Reischauer system and the newer Revised Romanization of Korean, which was introduced in 2000. This book uses Revised Romanization. Here are a few examples of place names in the two different systems:

McCune-Reischauer	Revised Romanization
Gwangju	Kwangju
Daegu	Taegu
Seongju	Sungju
Geumgok	Kumgok
Inchon	Incheon

TO FIND OUT MORE ABOUT THE LONG, COLORFUL HISTORY OF THE KOREA PENINSULA, GO TO WWW.INAMERICABOOKS.COM FOR LINKS.

According to legend, a hero named Dan–gun founded Korea in 2333 B.C. Dan–gun established his capital at Pyongyang and called his kingdom Chosun, "Land of the Morning Calm." While this ancient founding cannot be proven, written records show that native Korean kingdoms arose as early as 193 B.C. During this period, three powerful kingdoms were established: Koguryo in the North, and the kingdoms of Baekje and Silla in the South.

These kingdoms began trading goods, such as furs and spices, with the powerful neighboring empire of China. Business and political dealings led to an exchange of cultural ideas, and Chinese religious and philosophical systems were soon introduced to Korea. Among the most important of these was Buddhism, a religion established in India in the fifth century B.C. Many Chinese were Buddhists, followers of Buddhism, who believe that self–knowledge and meditation lead to enlightenment. Buddhism became the dominant religion in Korea, and Buddhist art, music, architecture, and culture quickly spread.

Korea also adopted Confucianism from China. Confucianism, a philosophy based on the teachings of the Chinese scholar Confucius, established a rigid system of social duties for each individual. It described the correct relationships between the rulers and the ruled, fathers and sons, husbands and wives, and the young and the old. Korean rulers used this philosophy as a basis for their governments.

By the end of the seventh century A.D., the kingdom of Silla had conquered Koguryo and Baekje, uniting the Korea Peninsula under a single ruling family, or dynasty. In A.D. 936, the Silla dynasty was replaced by the Koryo dynasty, and the modern name Korea is derived from the name of this dynasty. Although the Koryo dynasty ruled for only four centuries of Korea's long history, it left behind a rich legacy of artistic, scientific, and literary achievements.

THE CHOSUN DYNASTY

In 1392 the Chosun dynasty (sometimes called the Yi dynasty after its founder, General Yi Song-gye) rose to power in Korea. During the early years of this dynasty, Confucianism gained strength as Korea's guiding philosophy. The Chosun rulers believed that Confucianism would maintain the

At the Buddhist Bulguksa Temple in Gyeongju, sculptures of the four Heavenly Kings—one for each cardinal direction (north, south, east, and west)—are said to permit goodness to enter the temple but keep evil out. The eastern Heavenly King (left) and the southern Heavenly King (right) are shown here.

kingdom's stability by instituting rules of order and obedience.

Social status was extremely important under the Chosun dynasty. The highest class included the royal family. The next class included members of prominent families. These people worked as scholars and administrators. They also owned land. Members of this class were most often born into this social status. They lived apart from the lower classes and also dressed differently to distinguish themselves. Often upper-class members considered the lower classes inferior.

KOREAN WOMEN AND CONFUCIANISM

In Chosun-dynasty Korea, Confucian ideals strictly governed the behavior of women, who were regarded as inferior to men. Girls lived with their mother until they were married. Then they moved to their husband's house, where they were ruled by their mother-in-law. Women were expected to act much differently than men. A woman was dishonored if she committed *chilgo chiak*, seven evils. These evils were disobeying her in-laws, bearing no son, promiscuity, jealousy, carrying a hereditary disease, talking too much, or stealing. Violating any of these rules resulted in severe punishment, sometimes even death.

Confucius (551–479 B.C.)

The lower class was made up of several layers. Professionals, such as doctors, were at the top. Farmers and craftspeople made up the second layer of the lower class. Those who owned land had higher status than those who did not. At the bottom of the social system were slaves. Like the highest class, they too were born into their social condition. Many slaves worked as servants or farm laborers. Because people inherited their social position, they had little chance to move up or down within the system.

In 1637 the neighboring Chinese invaded Korea. The Chosun dynasty was still allowed to rule their kingdom, but they were forced to pay a tribute (money) to China, as well as swear loyalty to the Chinese ruler. China's influence over Korea grew significantly. However, the Chinese and Chosun rulers closed the country to other nations. Korea's rulers believed that isolation from foreign nations would secure their power and protect their culture.

When European merchants and missionaries tried to enter the country in the 1700s and 1800s, Korea virtually closed its borders to them. This action earned Korea the nickname "Hermit Kingdom." But despite this isolation, European science and technology did seep into Korea through China.

THE OPENING OF KOREA

By the mid–1800s, European powers and the United States were all eager to set up trade for silks and spices. They began to pressure Korea and China to open their borders to the world. Korean suspicion and dislike of these foreign powers grew as China's own troubles with these countries increased. After a devastating war with Great Britain, known as the First Opium War (1839—1842), China was forced to open trading posts to European merchants.

Severely weakened by war and internal unrest, China could no longer keep foreign influence out of Korea. Japan pressured Korea to open its doors to the West and forced several trade agreements on Korea in 1876. Soon after, the United States established political ties with Korea and began to send representatives and to conduct trade. Numerous traders from many other nations also arrived. During the next thirty years, many Western ideas and inventions were introduced to Koreans.

Because of these more open policies, laws forbidding Christian missionaries from entering Korea ended. Before, Christian missionaries who tried to spread their religion were often killed. But after 1876, missionaries were free to mingle with the people and try to persuade them to change their beliefs. At first, the missionaries were unsuccessful. The Koreans did not believe in a single god as Christians do, and they distrusted the foreigners. Before 1890 only a few Koreans were interested in converting to Christianity.

One important figure in Christianity's growth in Korea was Horace Newton Allen. Allen, an American missionary and doctor, arrived in Korea in 1884. He soon became a friend and adviser to Kojong, the nation's king. Kojong valued Allen's advice and permitted him to expand his missionary work.

*King Kojong ruled Korea from 1864 until 1907. In his later years in power, he sometimes wore Western clothing (**below**).*

Korea's opening also led to many other changes. Koreans began to travel to Japan and the United States, and many of them returned with new ideas about government and technology. Boats from foreign lands appeared at Korean ports, bringing not only foreigners but also foreign products. Construction began on railroads, linking the capital in Seoul with other important cities in Korea. English began to be taught in Korean schools, and Western social organizations, such as the YMCA, were established. Schools were set up to teach Western subjects, and many people began to wonder whether a democracy might be better than the monarchy (a government led by a single ruler such as a king) that they lived under.

In the 1890s, daily newspapers were first published in Korea. The first of these, *The Independent*, was established by Philip Jaisohn. Jaisohn, a Korean, had studied in the United States and had returned to Korea to help the country adopt more modern ways. Soon many other newspapers published stories about the people and customs of faraway lands. These changes meant that average Korean citizens began to think about the world that lay beyond their own little villages. Suddenly, they could read about— and even visit—these new lands.

Meanwhile, China clashed with Japan over control of Korea in 1894. Japanese troops then crossed Korea to attack China. Korean farmers and peasants rebelled, unsuccessfully, against this invasion. After Japan defeated China in 1895, Japanese troops remained in Korea. The Japanese took control of Korea's political and economic system. Japan also began changing the social fabric of the country. Although the Koreans resisted Japanese influence, the Koreans could not drive them out.

HARD TIMES

As the foreign influences in Korea increased, the country's political and economic systems faced several challenges. Discontent spread among the people as new ideas clashed with old customs. Many Korean families became poor and homeless during the Japanese occupation. International wars also created problems for the kingdom's economy, since it had grown dependent on outside markets. Forced to leave their farms in the countryside, people headed for the cities or seaports in search of work. Jobs were scarce, however, and the common people found themselves working harder and harder to satisfy the demands of corrupt officials. Many government workers taxed the people so heavily that the poorer people went into debt just to survive.

In early twentieth-century Korea, workers were so plentiful that it was cheaper for a lumberyard to hire laborers to cut lumber manually than to operate a mechanized sawmill.

Many of these troubled people turned to Christianity for answers and comfort. Some hoped that Christianity might offer a life free from the rigid social structure that trapped them in poverty. Others believed that, since Christianity was the predominant religion of Europe and the United States, turning to it might help Koreans modernize their nation.

Horace Allen saw how desperate many Koreans were, and he had an idea. Allen's friends included members of the Hawaiian Sugar Planters' Association in the United States. Sugarcane growers in Hawaii needed large numbers of laborers for their farms and plantations. They had hired many Chinese immigrants

Chinese laborers harvest Hawaiian sugarcane in the early 1900s.

THE KOREAN IS THE PICK OF ALL THE ORIENTALS AS A WORKMAN. I HAVE WORKED CHINESE, JAPANESE, AND KOREANS DURING THE PAST SEVEN YEARS, AND I HAVE NOT THE SLIGHTEST HESITATION IN SAYING THAT THE KOREAN IS DECIDEDLY THE BEST.

–a mining foreman on a Hawaiian sugarcane plantation in the 1920s

for this work, but new laws had temporarily ended Chinese immigration to the United States. The planters needed workers, and Koreans seemed like the perfect solution.

But getting workers was not so easy. King Kojong had allowed some citizens to emigrate (leave their homeland to move to another country), but the numbers remained very small. Knowing how influential Allen had become in Korea, the planters asked him for help. Allen tried to persuade the king, as well as the people.

For Koreans, the idea of emigrating to Hawaii—halfway across the Pacific Ocean—was very different from anything they had considered in the past. Some laborers had left Korea for work, but they usually moved to Russia or Japan—countries close to home. These Koreans could easily return to visit their families and their ancestors' graves to perform the ceremonies that Confucianism required. But as more people converted to Christianity, they began to consider

abandoning some of their ancient traditions and even settling in faraway lands.

The climate is suitable for everyone and there is no severe heat or cold. There are schools on every island. English is taught and the tuition is free. There are jobs available all year long for farmers who are healthy and decent in behavior. The monthly pay is $15. The work day is ten hours long and Sunday is free. Housing, fuel, water, and hospital expenses will be paid by the employer.

—recruiting poster from the early 1900s for Koreans to work at Hawaiian sugarcane plantations

KOREAN NAMES

Traditionally, Korean names appear with the family name first and the personal name last. Approximately half of all Koreans share common family names, such as Kim, Lee, or Chung.

Personal names generally have two parts, based on ancient symbols and family tradition. Korean males in the same family and in the same generation, brothers and male cousins, often share the same first part of the personal name. But the second part of their first name is different. For example, two brothers may be named Kim Jae Kyung and Kim Jae Hyung. For female Koreans, this rule is not as strictly followed. Female cousins do not have to share the same first part of their personal names, as their male counterparts do. However, sisters do often have the same first name.

When writing Korean names in English, the practice of putting the last name first is often continued. Some Korean Americans, however, have adopted the Western custom of placing the family name last.

Then, in 1901, a devastating drought hit Korea, followed by famine. The fields were bare, people were starving, and the future seemed bleak. Many farmers and villagers left their homes to look for work in the kingdom's cities. To help his people, Kojong agreed to Allen's requests for emigration to Hawaii. Feeling hopeless, desperate Koreans began thinking about starting over in a new land.

In 1902 a group of more than one hundred Korean emigrants decided to strike out for the United States. Nearly half of the people in this early group were Korean Christians. Many of them were from the northern part of the kingdom. Northerners had generally faced tougher conditions than those living on the southern half of the peninsula. The land in the North was harder to farm, border wars with neighboring countries had often occurred there, and the class system was much more rigid than in the South.

These Koreans had a common goal—to improve their lives. Recruiters told them that Hawaii was paradise and that America was a "land of dreams." America promised them hope that they did not have if they stayed in Korea.

The 1901 drought made this Korean farmer's load of hay more valuable, but he still had a hard life under Japanese rule. Many lower-class Koreans became willing to leave home for jobs in the United States.

2
MOVING TO AMERICA

That first wave of Korean immigrants began their journey to the United States on December 22, 1902. A group of 121 laborers, farmers, students, and political refugees boarded trains from many of the larger cities, such as Busan, Gampo, and Ulsan, along Korea's coast. They then boarded boats to travel across the Korea Strait to Japan. In Japan the Korean men cut their hair, traditionally worn long, and bought Western-style clothing. The emigrants then waited in Japan for large ships to transport them across the Pacific Ocean to the Hawaiian Islands.

THE JOURNEY

The journey to America was not easy. Many emigrants piled into the cramped quarters of the ships. Food was limited and of poor quality. The air was stale, and disease spread quickly.

During the trip, Christian missionaries and ministers tried to convert more emigrants to

Christianity, and many Koreans did convert to Christianity on the ships. The missionaries also taught them to speak and read some English before their arrival in America.

The group arrived in Hawaii on January 13, 1903, as the first of sixty-five shiploads of Koreans that would cross the Pacific over the next two years. Landing in Honolulu was exciting and scary. This would be the start of their new life. But most of the immigrants knew little English. They did not know what type of work they would be doing or how their bosses would treat them. They didn't know where they would live or what they would eat.

As soon as the immigrants stepped off the boat, doctors examined them. Many people found

Honolulu Harbor was the first glimpse of America that many early Korean immigrants had.

themselves quarantined, or separated from the others, because of illness or physical ailments. Some were even sent back to Korea. Healthy immigrants also waited in their own quarantine stations for several days to make sure they did not have diseases.

Once the doctors allowed the immigrants to leave, horse–drawn carts took them to large farms, called plantations. Some stayed on the island of Oahu. Others were transferred to smaller boats that transported them to one of the other Hawaiian islands, mainly Hawaii, Maui, Kauai, or Molokai. Their life in America had begun.

PLANTATION LIFE

Korean immigrants in Hawaii soon discovered that the next three years of their lives had been planned by the sugarcane planters. To pay for their trip to America, many Koreans had borrowed money from banks run by plantation owners. The planters took part of their workers' wages to pay off the loan. Planters also expected the immigrants to work at least three years on plantations.

As Hawaii's principal crop, sugarcane dominated immigrant life on the islands. The new field-workers lived in camps on the plantation. Families occupied small houses, while single men shared quarters in large, one-room barracks. Planters segregated their workers—Japanese, Chinese, and Koreans all lived in separate areas.

While planters provided housing, the immigrants were expected to pay for their food. Everyone was welcome to eat together in a big kitchen, and those who did paid $6.50 a month for all their meals. Those who wanted to could buy their own food and cook their own meals. Some of the immigrants formed a group to cook foods from their own countries.

Life on the plantation was difficult. Workers labored in the fields, under the hot sun, for ten hours a day. Often they rose at five in the morning, ate a quick breakfast, and then boarded trains to their assigned fields.

Korean immigrants' families lived in this row of houses on the Ewa plantation on the Hawaiian island of Oahu.

KIMCHI

Korean immigrants held on to their heritage through their cuisine. One favorite is Kimchi, the Koreas' national dish. Kimchi is made by pickling cabbage or cucumbers in salt, adding seasonings, and letting the mixture ferment. Kimchi also expresses Korean symbolism. Its five colors (green, red, white, black, and yellow) and flavors (salty, spicy, sour, sweet, and bitter) represent directions and seasons. Check out www.inanamericabooks.com for links to more Korean recipes.

5 C. GREEN OR CHINESE CABBAGE, CUT INTO BITE-SIZED PIECES

6 TSP. SALT

2 TBSP. SUGAR

1 TSP. TO 2 TBSP. CRUSHED RED PEPPER FLAKES

¼ TSP. PEELED AND FINELY CHOPPED GINGERROOT

1 CLOVE GARLIC, PEELED AND FINELY CHOPPED

2 GREEN ONIONS, FINELY CHOPPED

1. In a large colander, mix cabbage with 5 tsp. salt. Let stand three hours.
2. Rinse cabbage thoroughly two or three times. Gently squeeze out excess liquid with your hands.
3. Place the drained cabbage in a large glass or ceramic bowl. Add the final 1 tsp. salt and the rest of the ingredients. Mix thoroughly.
4. Cover cabbage mixture tightly with plastic wrap and let stand at room temperature for one or two days.
5. Chill kimchi before serving. Store tightly covered. Kimchi will keep indefinitely in the refrigerator.

Makes 5 cups

Field-workers took a half-hour break for lunch after a long morning. Then they worked until about 4:30 in the afternoon. They returned to camp by train, often going straight to bed after supper. During the harvest season, they worked seven days a week. Otherwise, the immigrants had Sunday off. They used their day off to visit with each other, go to church, or to sleep.

Many of the immigrants had not expected this kind of hard work in the "land of opportunity." Some were scholars and artisans, unused to fieldwork. And the pay was poor. Some plantation owners paid as little as eighteen dollars per month, although more generous

CHURCHES

For early Korean immigrants, churches became a strong foundation for their communities. Churches provided services and aid for new arrivals, such as housing information, language classes, and social events. Many Korean American churches, such as the Korean Christian Church in Hana, Maui, Hawaii *(below)*, even offered a family atmosphere as a substitute for the traditional extended Korean family.

The Korean women immigrants on the Kaeleku Sugar Plantation earned less than men as field-workers. The women also had a lot of family responsibilities.

owners paid their workers closer to forty dollars a month. The few women living on the plantations earned much less. Most women worked as cooks for the field-workers. Some even labored alongside the men in the field, often with their infant children strapped to their backs. They earned about fifteen to seventeen dollars a month. In the evenings, they returned to camp to wash and iron the workers' clothes to earn extra money. Many women living on plantations slept only about four hours each night.

Lunas, or camp foremen, received nearly twice what the average field-worker made. Most lunas were white men, although some immigrants were also chosen to oversee the workers. Lunas typically managed about 250 workers, watching closely to make sure everyone followed the rules. These included no talking, no smoking, and no stretching stiff backs. Breaking the rules might result in physical punishment, especially whipping.

While most immigrants made little money, it was still more than many had made in Korea. And the immigrants working on the plantations had very few expenses. Many sent money home to their families. Others saved it, hoping to go back to Korea a little better off.

Returning to their homeland remained a goal for most of the early Korean immigrants. Few actually accomplished this, however. Between 1903 and 1905, approximately seven thousand Korean immigrants arrived to labor on the Hawaiian sugar plantations. Of this number, only about two thousand were able to go home. The rest remained in America for the rest of their lives.

PROBLEMS IN PARADISE

Plantation owners favored Asian laborers over other ethnic groups because they were usually willing to work for lower wages. But many Hawaiian townspeople disliked and distrusted the immigrants. Korean immigrants were equally suspicious of the Westerners, and distrust between Japanese and Korean immigrants proved to be a problem. Japan had come to occupy Korean territory, a fact most Koreans deeply resented, and strong rivalries existed between these two immigrant groups in America, as well.

Some planters used this tension to their advantage. Japanese workers made up the largest ethnic group on the plantations. But they frequently protested against the shabby working conditions and low wages, often going on strike (refusing to work). Many planters then hired Koreans, who were still willing to work, to fill in

TO FIND OUT MORE ABOUT KOREAN IMMIGRANTS' EXPERIENCES IN THE UNITED STATES, GO TO WWW.INAMERICABOOKS.COM FOR LINKS.

27

for their Japanese laborers. This lessened the effectiveness of the Japanese strikes, leaving both immigrant groups powerless. In turn, this further aggravated the existing tension between the groups.

Health problems also plagued the immigrants living on the plantations. Infectious diseases spread quickly through close living quarters. While plantations provided free medical care, most of the doctors did not speak Korean. Immigrants had trouble explaining their symptoms or understanding a doctor's advice. And the hard fieldwork left many able-bodied workers aching, severely sunburned, and undernourished.

Soonkee Rhee **(standing, center, wearing white)** *was an interpreter for Korean laborers on the Hawaiian islands of Oahu and Maui in the early twentieth century. Labor disputes and Korean immigrants' health problems kept interpreters busy.*

BUILDING A COMMUNITY

To improve their lives on the plantations, Korean immigrants established their own community. Several organizations and practices helped the immigrants adjust to life in a strange land with foreign customs. One of the most important was the *donghoe,* or a community council. The donghoe was headed by a mayor, who was elected once a year and who enforced the laws of the community. He could arrest and fine any Korean who broke the rules. The council was also

designed to handle the problems that occasionally arose in rough plantation life, such as gambling, fighting, and drinking.

A second type of organization grew out of the Korean Christians' strong ties with the Church. The Church had helped take care of the new Korean immigrants when they'd first arrived. In 1903 Korean Christians founded the Korean Evangelical Society, later called the Korean Methodist Church. The Church helped organize a language school to teach English to the workers. The Church also sometimes conducted religious services in Korean to help new

A KOREAN MOTHER'S ADVICE

Dear boy, I hear foreigners don't use rice. I can't imagine how anybody could live without eating rice three times a day. When I think how hungry you must be on cakes made of some kind of flour, I can neither sleep nor eat. Don't you, even for fun, put on foreign clothes. Oh, how ugly a foreigner appears in tight black trousers looking like a pair of walking stilts. My son, I hear that Korean youths who go abroad contract the bad habit of smoking cigarettes instead of our long pipes and of loving foreign costumes, despising the topknot [traditional Korean male hairstyle of looping one's hair on top of one's head], and the beautiful Korean dress and hats of large dimensions. I cannot explain this change of heart otherwise than supposing that when a Korean goes abroad, foreigners give him a certain medicine to change him.

—an early twentieth-century letter from a Korean mother to her son in the United States

immigrants participate in church activities. The church became an important social and cultural center for the Korean community.

Another practice of the Korean immigrant community was to help ambitious workers set up their own businesses. Working on plantations usually did not pay enough for someone to start a business, and banks would not loan money to Korean workers. Therefore, to raise the necessary money, an immigrant would turn to Korean friends, who would pool some of their money in a fund called a *gye*. An entrepreneur could use the gye to set up a small business and pay back the borrowed money later. Many Korean immigrants were able to become independent business owners through this system.

Korean immigrants also established their communities by creating schools for their children. These schools taught children about the Korean language and culture. Proud of their ancient history and customs, Korean immigrants wanted their Hawaiian–born children to understand and appreciate their heritage. This also ensured that the Korean culture would endure, even outside their homeland. Parents paid schoolteachers out of their own meager wages.

The teachers and students of the Korean Christian Institute in Hawaii pose for a photo in the early twentieth century. Dr. Syngman Rhee (**fourth from left**), *the future president of South Korea, is one of the teachers.*

THE FIRST MIGRATION ENDS

At first, Korean immigration to Hawaii went smoothly. But problems began to arise. Some Korean officials objected to the emigration because of the working conditions for Koreans in Hawaii. Some claimed that Korean workers had been "sold into slavery."

In addition, Japan defeated Russia in a struggle to control Korea in 1905. Japan extended its influence into the inner circles of the Korean government. Opposed to Koreans going to Hawaii and competing with Japanese workers, the Japanese began looking for an excuse to force the government to prohibit emigration.

The Japanese soon found their excuse. In January 1905, a new emigration company persuaded about one thousand Koreans to go to Mexico as laborers on hemp farms. (Hemp is used to make rope.) A few months later, a Korean merchant discovered that the laborers worked under slavelike conditions and immediately notified the Korean government. That same day, the Japanese government prohibited all Korean emigration to both Mexico and Hawaii.

In November 1905, the Japanese forced Korea to become a protectorate (a dependent state). Under Japanese rule, Korea experienced widespread economic development and modernization. Updated farming methods were introduced, and factories sprang up in the North. These advances did little to improve the lives of average Koreans, however. Many Korean farmers were forced off their land, which was given over to Japanese industry. Japan took half of Korea's rice

crop for its own use, creating huge food shortages
for Koreans.

The Japanese also controlled Korean schools and
businesses. They forced Koreans to speak Japanese at
school and at work and to adopt Japanese names.
Korean newspapers and political groups were banned.
Koreans were not allowed to follow their own
religion, either.

Japan was also in charge of all of Korea's foreign
affairs. The Japanese government prohibited Korean
emigration. For Koreans in America, with foreigners
ruling their land, there was no home to go back to.

LEAVING THE PLANTATIONS

Korean immigrants in the United States knew that
America might become their permanent home. Most
realized that they had three real choices. They could
continue their backbreaking work on the plantations,
they could move into the cities of Hawaii, or they
could move to the U.S. mainland.

Most knew that working on the sugarcane
plantations was not the life for them. Plantation work
presented no real future. They had stayed on the
plantations, at first, because they had no other choice,
for they needed to work off their loans to the
plantation owners. But once they had fulfilled their
contracts with the planters, Korean immigrants, by and
large, began to look for new work.

Many Korean immigrants decided to leave the
plantations but to stay in Hawaii. They looked for work

A Korean field-worker and ox plow a rocky Hawaiian hillside. Plantation work was grueling. Many Korean immigrants looked for other kinds of work in Hawaii and on the U.S. mainland.

in the cities, especially in Honolulu. But racism against Asian immigrants still existed. Most Korean immigrants did not speak English very well yet or understand American customs. This made it difficult to find work off of the plantations. White business owners often refused to hire Asians for the better-paying jobs. Because of this, many Koreans decided to set up their own businesses using the gye system. Koreans soon became launderers, shoe repair workers, furniture store owners, apartment caretakers, tailors, and grocers. They eventually developed Koreatowns, ethnic communities where Korean immigrants owned the stores, banks, churches, and schools.

Other Koreans who left the plantations decided to move to the U.S. mainland. About one thousand boarded boats to the West Coast.

Many settled in California, Oregon, and Washington, working in orchards, on vegetable farms, and on railroads. Here, too, some Koreans successfully established their own businesses. Others took unskilled jobs as busboys and servers in restaurants and hotels, and as janitors or gardeners—despite their educational or professional training.

Yet discrimination against Asians existed on the mainland too. Employers paid Asian immigrants less than their non–Asian coworkers, and few opportunities existed for promotions. Many white landlords refused to rent homes to Koreans, leaving the immigrants to look for housing in poorer neighborhoods. White laborers feared that Asian immigrants, who typically worked for less pay, would take work away from them. Korean immigrants were refused service at many restaurants and other public establishments. And the mainland Korean communities remained small, so Korean immigrants could not develop

Koreatowns to establish a strong ethnic community.

Korean students faced discrimination in school. White students and even teachers often

I felt the discrimination and realized that America was not a free country. Everybody did not enjoy liberty. The American people saw the Asian people as a different race. They didn't respect the Asian people. I wanted some postal or factory work, but they didn't give it to me. I couldn't get a job.

—Sa-sun Whang, a Korean immigrant to the United States, discussing discrimination in the 1920s

A Korean laborer at an early twentieth-century workers' camp in California leans on his hoe for a rest. Korean immigrants worked hard, but they were not prepared for the social isolation they experienced on the U.S. mainland.

ridiculed Asian students. Koreans were lumped together with other Asian minorities, such as Chinese, Japanese, and Filipino, and were frequently called insulting names. Some Koreans even became the victims of violence by white gangs.

The U.S. government also targeted Koreans. Many powerful groups tried to keep Asian immigrants, including Koreans, from moving to the United States. In 1907 President Theodore Roosevelt banned the immigration of all Asians to the U.S. mainland.

Japan annexed (officially took control of) Korea in 1910. This affected Korean immigrants, who were formally forbidden by the Japanese government to return to their homeland. Yet the U.S. government did not permit them to become U.S. citizens. In 1913 California passed a law stating that only white immigrants and U.S. citizens could own land, leaving Korean immigrants with even fewer options. (About two–thirds of the Korean immigrant population on the mainland lived in California, particularly San Francisco and Los Angeles.) But the Korean minority was simply too small to fight back. And because they were not citizens, most Koreans could not vote to change the laws.

Theodore Roosevelt was president of the United States from 1901 to 1909.

KOREAN IMMIGRANTS IN AMERICA

WASHINGTON

MINNESOTA

OREGON

NEW YORK

Minneapolis
Rochester

New York City

San Francisco
Reedley

Chicago

ILLINOIS

Washington, D.C.

CALIFORNIA

Los Angeles

MEXICO

HAWAIIAN ISLANDS

OAHU

Ewa

KAUAI

MAUI

Pearl Harbor

Honolulu
and Honolulu Harbor

Hana

MOLOKAI

HAWAII

This map of Korean American population centers and other maps are downloadable at www.inamericabooks.com.

BETWEEN TWO CULTURES

Like other immigrants to America, the first wave of Korean immigrants tried to preserve their old way of life in their new land. They spoke the Korean language, ate Korean food, and preserved many habits and customs of everyday life practiced in the old country.

Students from the Korean Girls Seminary in Hawaii made a float for the Mid-Pacific Carnival parade in February 1917. They wore traditional Korean clothing for the event. Carnival celebrates Fat Tuesday, a Christian holiday that comes before Ash Wednesday and Easter. Historically, Korean Americans have worn Korean clothing for special occasions in both cultures.

One such custom was the continued observance of traditional Korean holidays, such as the king's birthday. These occasions called for grand feasts with much singing, dancing, eating, and drinking. At these feasts, a traditional separation of the sexes was strictly observed. Men and women sat apart from each other when they ate, and women did not join in the singing and dancing because it was considered improper. But these gala occasions did give Korean women a rare opportunity to dress in their finest traditional gowns, made from brightly colored Korean silks.

Korean immigrants tried to preserve traditional habits and customs in everyday affairs as well as ceremonial occasions. When sleeping, they used hard pillows made from blocks of wood instead of sleeping on soft feather pillows, and they ate with chopsticks instead of with forks. And although the men often wore American–style clothes, many women continued to wear traditional Korean dress.

Many social customs also continued. As was the practice in Korea, following the guidelines of Confucianism, respect was always given to older people. Youngsters had to be polite, even to their older brothers, sisters, and cousins. When illness struck, the Korean immigrants usually relied on their own traditional medicine, based on acupuncture and Asian herbs, instead of turning to American doctors.

One of the most important means of preserving the old way of life was by marrying within the Korean community. Because few Korean women lived in America, male immigrants used the "picture bride system" to obtain wives. A man's family back in Korea would contact a matchmaker for him. Then the matchmaker and the groom's family selected women who might be willing to move to America.

Many young women in Korea hoped to improve their lives. Some agreed to become picture brides to escape economic hardships and Japanese rule. Others believed that in America they would find more opportunities for education and careers, which were rather limited in their homeland. For most, the picture bride system seemed like a chance for a new life in a new land.

Once a woman expressed interest in emigrating, she gave a photograph of herself to the matchmaker. She then received a photo of her would–be husband. If both the immigrant and the woman's family agreed, the man sent his bride about one hundred dollars for traveling expenses. When she arrived in America, they married right on the docks. That way, the woman could legally enter the United States. This system brought wives to America for many Korean men between 1910 and 1924.

What the picture brides didn't know was that many of the immigrants had sent old pictures of themselves to seem younger than they really were. Worse, the immigrants often exaggerated how much money they had. Consequently, when the picture brides arrived in America and first met their intended husbands face-to-face, some were greatly disappointed. Despite such disappointments, about one thousand Korean women entered the United States in this way before the immigration laws changed in 1924, severely restricting Korean immigration to the United States. The new limits ensured that the Korean immigrant population remained small. Nearly three decades and two wars ended before the second major wave of Korean immigrants began.

WHEN I FIRST SAW MY FIANCÉ, I COULD NOT BELIEVE MY EYES. HIS HAIR WAS GREY AND I COULD NOT SEE ANY RESEMBLANCE TO THE PICTURE I HAD. I DEFINITELY LOOKED ON HIM MORE AS MY FATHER THAN MY HUSBAND.

—Anna Choi, a Korean picture bride, 1915

MAKING IT ON THE MAINLAND

In Reedley, California, two friends named Kim formed a large-scale farming business in 1921. Their company developed a new type of fruit, the nectarine, and eventually became a multimillion-dollar enterprise. Five years later, Peter Hyon established the Oriental Food Products Company of California. This business venture also enjoyed great success. Besides these large firms, many other smaller Korean businesses thrived in California.

By 1940 more than thirty Korean fruit and vegetable stands, nine groceries, eight laundries, six trucking companies, five wholesalers, five restaurants, three drugstores, two hat shops, one employment agency, and one rooming house operated in the Los Angeles area alone.

The Korean American Chun family (behind the counter) *ran a lunchroom on Kedzie Avenue in Chicago, Illinois, for many years. This photograph was taken in 1931.*

3

BECOMING KOMERICAN

Life in America became more difficult for almost everyone in the 1930s, when serious economic problems led to the Great Depression. Koreans were hit especially hard because most had large families to support. Many small businesses struggled to stay open. Farms and plantations throughout the nation suffered from devastating droughts, leaving many farm laborers desperate for work. Korean immigrants continued to work hard to carve out a life in their adopted home.

FINDING A PLACE

A generation gap and a changing sense of identity presented challenges for Koreans living in America during these early years. Although Korean immigrants tried to hold onto their own identity in America, their small numbers made this very hard. The mainland Korean population, especially, was too small to create Koreatowns in the cities in which they had settled.

Two Korean Americans stop in front of Yim's ice cream parlor in Los Angeles in 1938. This city has always had the highest number of Korean Americans on the U.S. mainland. Elsewhere, Korean Americans faced more pressure to get along with neighbors from other ethnic groups.

Instead, Koreans lived in neighborhoods composed of many different races and nationalities. They learned English in order to communicate with their neighbors. They began to abandon many of their Korean-style clothes and customs, becoming "Americanized" much more quickly than other, larger Asian immigrant groups.

This rapid rate of Americanization often caused problems in Korean family life. Korean immigrants experienced high rates of divorce and juvenile delinquency. And many families struggled to create a new identity, one that included both their Korean background and their American home. These identity issues grew more complicated as these immigrants had children. Their children, born in the United States, were U.S. citizens by birth. But these U.S.-born children found many differences between their Korean-born parents and themselves.

The first-generation immigrants maintained strong ties to their homeland. To instill a strong Korean heritage in their children, they sent them to special schools to learn about the Korean language and customs. Korean-culture camps were also started so Korean American children could learn more about Korea's history and traditions.

But because of the small Korean American population, there was not much money to support the early cultural schools. Many did not last long. Korean children, like the children of the other immigrant groups, considered themselves Americans. They had never seen Korea, and therefore they felt no ties to their parents' native land. They also felt that speaking Korean would make them less American. They preferred to use the English language and to adopt American customs. Their parents, on the other hand, felt that their children's reluctance to use the Korean language showed a lack of respect for their elders and for Korean culture.

As the first-generation immigrants grew older and approached retirement, they wanted their children to join the struggle for Korean independence from Japan. But many young Korean Americans believed that, as Americans, they need not be involved in the affairs of a foreign country, not even the land of their parents' birth.

As the second generation grew up, many Korean Americans found their parents' social customs and traditional ways of doing things old-fashioned. As the second generation entered adulthood, they began to attend college and to climb the ladder of success. They also began to marry people of other races, as well. Because of such intermarriage, their own ethnic identity became blurred. Korean Americans who belonged to Christian churches chose to have Western-style weddings and to wear American clothing instead of following the traditional ways.

GENERATION 1.5

Koreans who are born in Korea but who move to America with their immigrant parents are known as 1.5 generation Korean Americans. The term was coined by Korean Americans to differentiate between those Koreans born in Korea and those born in America. (American-born Korean Americans are sometimes called the 2.0 generation.) Members of the 1.5 generation are comfortable with both Korean and American customs. They speak both Korean and English, and they are more likely than first-generation immigrants to feel at home in American culture.

A NATION AT WAR

Japanese forces attacked Pearl Harbor, Hawaii, on December 7, 1941. Shortly after the attack, the United States declared war on Japan and entered World War II. Korean immigrants supported the war, believing that if America defeated the Japanese, Korea might again be a free nation. To help, some who knew Japanese taught the language to U.S. soldiers or translated Japanese letters and documents into English.

Korean Americans contributed to the war effort in other ways. They donated money, volunteered to fight, and publicly expressed their support. Despite these efforts, Americans seemed uncertain how to treat Korean immigrants. Because Korea remained a Japanese protectorate, Americans turned a suspicious eye on Korean Americans during the early part of the war. In 1942 U.S. president Franklin D. Roosevelt ordered Japanese immigrants and their families to move to guarded camps in California, Oregon, and Washington, even if they were U.S. citizens. Because Koreans were still

A Korean American U.S. Army Reserve unit in California poses for a photograph in 1942.

mistaken for Japanese—a mistake considered an insult in itself by Koreans—some were also sent to these relocation camps. In Hawaii, Americans labeled both Japanese and Korean immigrants as enemy aliens, forcing them to obey a curfew, requiring them to stay home from dusk until dawn. Violating curfew resulted in fines or even jail.

Koreans tried to distinguish themselves from the Japanese. Many Korean women in Hawaii began to wear their traditional clothing to emphasize that they were not Japanese.

Korean efforts to help in the war and to support the United States eventually paid off. Many white Americans began to see Korean immigrants in a new light. In 1944 congressional representatives worked to pass a law that would allow Korean immigrants to become U.S. citizens. While the law did not pass, it was an important step forward in the fight to gain American acceptance.

THE KOREAN WAR

World War II ended in August 1945. Japan had been defeated, and Korea was finally free of Japanese control. Yet the Japanese defeat brought new problems to Korea. At the war's end, the Soviet Union (a union of fifteen republics in eastern Europe and Asia, including Russia) sent troops into the northern part of Korea, while U.S. forces controlled the southern part. The Soviet Union was led by a Communist government. This type of government controls all aspects of a country's economy, including the means and production of goods and services. The Soviet Union wanted Communism to expand across Asia. The United States believed that this expansion of Communism would hurt U.S. trade and foreign relations. These two superpowers each wanted to establish their own type of government in Korea.

A temporary division of Korea resulted and continued for years, despite efforts to reunite the country. Eventually, two separate governments took shape in Korea. In the North, Kim Il Sung introduced a Communist government. At the same time, South Korea elected a non–Communist leader, Syngman Rhee. Rhee had been educated in the United States.

After World War II, Korean immigration to America almost completely stopped. South Korea discouraged emigration to the United States, and North Korea did not allow any kind of emigration. A quota system set by the U.S. government further restricted the flow of immigrants, allowing only 150

TO READ MORE ABOUT KOREAN AMERICANS' ROLES IN AMERICA'S WARS, GO TO WWW.INAMERICABOOKS.COM FOR LINKS.

immigrants from each Asian nation into the United States each year. Those few immigrants usually had technical training, specialized skills, or college educations.

In June 1950, North Korea attacked South Korea, sparking the Korean War. U.S. troops rushed in to help South Korea, fearing the spread of Communism in Asia. But when U.S. forces began to penetrate close to the Chinese border in the North, China—also a Communist country— entered the war on the side of the North Koreans.

MANY PEOPLE ARE INTERESTED IN LEARNING ABOUT THEIR FAMILY'S HISTORY. THIS STUDY IS CALLED GENEALOGY. IF YOU'D LIKE TO LEARN ABOUT YOUR OWN GENEALOGY AND HOW YOUR ANCESTORS CAME TO AMERICA, VISIT WWW.INAMERICABOOKS.COM FOR TIPS AND LINKS TO HELP YOU GET STARTED.

The Korean War ended with no decisive winner, leaving the Korea Peninsula devastated and killing an estimated one million civilians. In 1953 the Soviet Union and the United States agreed to permanently divide Korea in two. These two Koreas had separate governments, Communism in the North and democracy in the South. The United States signed a treaty with the South Korean government allowing U.S. soldiers to be stationed in South Korea. About fifty thousand Americans stayed in Korea after the war. Americans became a common sight in South Korea.

Many U.S. soldiers stationed in Korea met and dated local Korean women, and some fell in love with them. Some soldiers married their Korean sweethearts and brought them to America. These women were called "war brides," and they became part of the second major wave of Korean immigration to the United States. An estimated one in four present-day Korean Americans trace their roots back to war brides.

War brides faced their own unique challenges. Interracial marriage was frowned upon both in Korea and in the United States. Korean society traditionally considered marriage an important family affair, usually arranged by the parents of the bride and groom. Often the families and backgrounds of an intended couple were regarded as more important to a successful marriage than love was. For many Korean women who chose to marry U.S. servicemen, the responses of their family and villages were negative.

Once they moved to America, most war brides still faced strong prejudice and social discrimination against interracial marriages. For many of these Korean women, moving to a new land with a foreign social structure and different customs—far beyond the support of their family and friends—proved very difficult. They did their best to adjust, however. Some joined the workforce, often in service and retail industries, while others stayed home to raise their children.

A Korean war bride (left) *washes dishes with her European American mother-in-law.*

One improvement for Korean immigrants was a law allowing Asians living in the United States, including Koreans, to become citizens. For the first time, Koreans in the United States had the same rights as other Americans. War brides, therefore, became Korean Americans.

Meanwhile, Korean children also immigrated to America after the

> *Mixed-blood children (Korean and American) were often mistreated by people (in Korea) who hated them because of their tainted heritage. Many were abandoned by their mothers and either entered a life of slavery or lived on the streets, begging or stealing for food.*
>
> *—Elizabeth Kim, a post-Korean War orphan in the 1960s*

Korean War. Some of these South Korean children had been born to U.S. servicemen and Korean women, while others had been orphaned by the war. For those children left without homes and families, U.S. adoption agencies found foster homes in the United States. Most orphans eventually found American families to adopt them as their own. Between 1950 and 1964, roughly fourteen thousand Koreans, mostly war brides and orphans, entered the United States.

New Immigrants and Old Problems

In 1965 and again in 1968, U.S. immigration laws changed, each time allowing more Koreans to enter the country. America once again seemed to be a land of opportunity. The Korean economy still lay in ruins, and the country remained weakened by years of war. People faced poverty and starvation. Rebuilding seemed to move too slowly. For many, the United States presented a more secure future.

Many North Koreans, including scholars and professionals, wanted to defect, or flee, from the harsh new government. Although North Korea was a closed society and did not allow its people to leave, people managed to escape to South Korea. Some defectors then immigrated to the United States.

This led to the third wave of Korean immigrants. Soon the number of Koreans immigrating to the United States each year shot up to about fifteen thousand. Many were professionals seeking better job prospects. Doctors, nurses, engineers, scientists, and other well-trained Koreans believed that the United States' stronger economy could provide them with a better quality of life for them and their children. As more and more Koreans left their homeland, the South Korean government began to fear the loss of its most talented people. The government soon limited the number of people who could leave South Korea. North Korea still did not officially allow its people to leave.

Although the third wave of immigrants had, overall, more education and training than the earlier Korean immigrants, they faced similar challenges. Like the first wave, language, cultural differences, and lack of money plagued their entry into American society. These factors deterred even trained professionals. Many had to take semiskilled work that paid less than their professions. For example, a college professor might work as a cab driver or at a store.

Discrimination also haunted the new Korean immigrants, just as it had plagued earlier waves.

> AMERICA IS MY COUNTRY. I CONSIDER MYSELF AN AMERICAN BORN IN KOREA. AS AN AMERICAN, I WANT TO LIVE IN HARMONY WITH OTHER AMERICANS. I HAVE HOPE FOR AMERICA.
>
> —*Sung Yong Park, a Korean who immigrated to the United States with his family in 1976*

RETURNING TO KOREA

Not all Korean immigrants to the United States stayed. In fact, since the 1980s, roughly forty thousand Korean immigrants in the United States have returned to Korea. This is not a new pattern for Korean immigrants. Many first-generation immigrants, those who moved to Hawaii's plantations, had originally hoped to return to their homeland once they had made enough money. But after the Japanese took over Korea, they had to stay in the United States.

As South Korea underwent political and economic reforms, in the 1970s and 1980s, it once again became a more stable country. Because of these reforms and the problems some immigrants faced in their adopted land, more and more Koreans decided to move back to Korea.

Koreans still were at the mercy of prejudiced landlords and employers. And new racial slurs also taunted them. For many, opportunities seemed scarce.

To combat job discrimination, many Koreans followed the lead of earlier immigrants and went into business for themselves. They opened restaurants, stores, and other small businesses around the country. But for many well-educated Korean professionals—doctors, professors, engineers, and pharmacists—working in these stores instead of in their fields was exhausting and degrading. Still, many felt that owning their own businesses was the best way to make life better for their families.

By the mid–1970s, more than 1,200 Korean businesses operated in America. Most were very small and employed only a few people. But with a strong work ethic and success as business owners, Korean immigrants began to earn the respect of their American neighbors.

Owning a small business was not easy, however. Korean shopkeepers relied on their families to help run their businesses.

Children often helped their parents in the store before and after school. The family worked hard, with parents often putting in as many as sixteen hours each day. Most Korean parents did so without complaint, believing that their sacrifice would help their children. A common goal for Korean Americans, who had been professionals in Korea, was to send their children to college to become professionals too.

A Korean American grocer checks the stock in his Los Angeles store. More than one thousand Korean American small businesses thrived across the United States in the 1970s.

By the early 1980s, the third wave of immigrants had raised the Korean population of the United States to approximately 700,000. Most Korean Americans lived in large cities, such as San Francisco, New York, Chicago, Honolulu, and Washington, D.C. But Los Angeles still housed the largest Korean American community. In fact, outside of Korea itself, Los Angeles contains the largest population of Koreans in the world.

Los Angeles's prosperous Koreatown has the U.S. mainland's largest population of Korean Americans in the early twenty-first century.

Korean life in Los Angeles during the 1980s grew along the city's Olympic Boulevard. This five-square-mile area became the largest Koreatown in the United States. Large numbers of Koreatown business owners encouraged the growth of a strong Korean identity in the neighborhood. It offered new immigrants a safe haven. In Koreatown the immigrants who spoke little or no English could communicate in their native tongue. They could retain their customs and history without fear of losing their ethnic identity or becoming too Americanized.

But Koreatown also kept these immigrants from venturing into American society. Many of those who lived in Koreatown never learned English or adopted American customs, restricting their acceptance in mainstream American culture. This separate community sometimes created tension between Korean immigrants and other minority groups, particularly African Americans.

Many outside groups believed that Korean shop owners treated them unfairly, overcharging for their goods or refusing to employ non–Koreans. Some resented the seemingly quick success of these new businesses. Korean business owners were blamed for the economic distress of other inner–city communities.

Tensions between Los Angeles's Koreatown residents and their neighbors escalated in the late 1980s and turned violent in 1992. On April 29, 1992, the African American community in Los Angeles rioted after a jury released four white police officers in the beating of a black motorist. Angry mobs broke into shops and set fire to buildings in Los Angeles. Many of these businesses belonged to Korean Americans. Some Korean Americans lost everything in

In April 1992, Los Angeles rioters burned down many small businesses owned by Korean Americans.

the riots. Koreans remember the day as *sa-i-gu* (Korean for "four twenty–nine"—April 29).

Many Korean Americans believed that they had been targeted during the riots because they had held too tightly to their ethnic identity. Some Koreatown leaders urged Korean Americans to become part of the larger community. One way was to hire workers outside of their families.

Korean organizations worked to bring minority groups together. For example, the Black–Korean Alliance in Los Angeles and the Korea Society in New York founded programs to promote understanding between the two groups. The goal of these organizations was to teach each group about both cultures. In 1993 Korea Society launched the Kids to Korea program, enabling sixteen African American high school students to travel to South Korea to learn more about its people and history. Project Bridge in Washington, D.C., began offering classes in Korean and African American culture. Groups such as the Legal Center worked to end hate crimes against Asians in America.

These groups further strengthened the community by promoting voter turnout. By exercising the right to vote, Koreans in America found a larger voice in the government. This helps

> *After the riots [of 1992], the 1.5 and 2.0 generations became much more aware and proud of what their parents went through, and the [first-generation] immigrants were grateful to the young Korean Americans' ethnic identity and activism. . . . many younger Koreans have come back to the community.*
>
> —Edward T. Chang, a Korean American professor

At a celebration of Korean culture in New York, two Korean American girls proudly dress in traditional Korean clothing and display an American flag.

them in the effort to protect their rights and to stop job and education discrimination.

GROWING UP KOMERICAN

Most Korean Americans born in the United States consider themselves Korean and American. These Korean Americans accept both cultures as their own. Instead of simply blending into mainstream American life, young Korean Americans strive to integrate their Korean traditions and heritage with their American way of life. This practice has created an entirely new identity for the children of Korean immigrants. The word *Komerican*, a combination of the words Korean and American, refers to members of these later generations. This term gives them their own identity, tying their traditional Korean customs to their American home.

Komericans want to find their voices—politically and culturally. They want to keep their Korean heritage while developing their American style. Many members of this group work hard in school. After they graduate from high school and college, they work in a variety of fields. These young Korean Americans are exploring the world outside of Koreatowns and contributing to a wide variety of fields. Komericans work in the entertainment industry, the fine arts, computer and information technology fields, medicine, and more.

As adults, the Korean children adopted by American families during and after the Korean War are also striving to find their place. These Komericans were raised by white American families but are making efforts to learn more about their Korean roots. Many grown-up war orphans have returned to Korea to visit their birthplace and to find

SPECIAL EVENTS

Korean American holidays are a good example of the blending of cultures. Some of these events are steeped in Korean heritage, while for others, American customs are taking over. For example, many modern Korean Americans choose to have American-style wedding ceremonies, complete with bridal gowns and tuxedos.

Celebrating a child's first birthday, on the other hand, often follows more traditional Korean rituals. The child is dressed in Korean costume and seated amidst rice cakes, fruit, and cookies. Friends and relatives show the child different objects that represent different careers. The first one the child picks up is said to be the child's future career.

relatives from their birth families. In 1999 adopted Komericans planned the first national conference for Korean American war orphans and their families. The conference reached out to more than 100,000 Korean Americans.

The newest generation of Komericans remains a small but strong community. They more easily straddle the line between their cultures than their parents or grandparents did, accepting both mainstream America and their Korean heritage.

Korean American artist Yong-Soon Min created this self-portrait. A kind of family tree grows from her mouth. Its branches are pieces of maps. A collage of family snapshots and photographs of world leaders are its leaves.

Komericans also care about what's going on in Korea. North Korea, in particular, attracted much attention and controversy in the late 1900s and early 2000s. Its government has been accused of developing nuclear weapons and of regularly violating the human rights of its citizens. In addition, in the early twenty–first century, the nation struggles with drought, flooding, and famine. Hoping to help the country, the Korean American community overwhelmingly turned out to support the North Korea Human Rights Act, which became law in 2004. It calls for sending humanitarian aid, such as food and medical supplies, to

North Korea. The act also seeks to end human rights abuses and to help North Korean refugees. Passage of this bill is just one example of how strong and unified the Korean American community is becoming.

Korean American drummers perform at a rally in New York. Many Korean Americans take a special interest in the issue of nuclear weapons since North Korea's secret nuclear energy program potentially threatens South Korea and the United States as well as its own people.

A STRONG COMMUNITY LOOKING AHEAD

In the early twenty-first century, Komericans around the United States celebrated the one-hundred-year anniversary of the first Korean immigrants' arrival in America. As a strong and growing group, they have much to celebrate. Despite this progress, however, Korean Americans still sometimes face the same hardships that the first immigrants faced. Some Korean American workers still struggle with poor housing and poor job opportunities. Racism, while less common, still affects some Korean Americans, especially those who do not speak English well. Some also face an ongoing struggle to gain the trust and respect of their American neighbors.

For many Korean Americans, adapting their traditional ideals to liberal American life also creates friction. Older Korean immigrants may still expect their children to marry a Korean and to follow long-standing traditions. For the younger generations, who often take pride in their Korean background but prefer to be more "American," these expectations may prove to be an unwelcome challenge. Bridging the gap between the Koreatowns and mainstream society will take time. While Korean Americans have made strides in this direction, more work needs to be done.

Nevertheless, the Korean American community is strong and growing. And with a population of more than one million, Komericans are becoming increasingly visible. They contribute to many areas of American society, from business to medicine to the arts. Korean Americans are doctors, engineers, business owners, and scholars. This young and dynamic group has promoted an understanding among Asian Americans and non–Asians through strong community organizations. Despite the challenges that still lie ahead, the future of Korean Americans looks bright.

In the early 2000s, a Korean American couple in Minneapolis, Minnesota, celebrated their marriage twice—with a Western wedding (left) *and with a Korean wedding* (right, bride in red and groom in blue). *Others were free to dress either way that day.*

FAMOUS KOREAN AMERICANS

DANA TAI SOON BURGESS (b.

1968) Dana Tai Soon Burgess is a dancer who founded the Moving Forward Dance Company in Washington, D.C. Burgess has received national recognition for his ability to combine Asian and Western dance styles and for his modern choreography. His work has been presented at and commissioned by the Smithsonian Institution, the John F. Kennedy Center for the Performing Arts, and the United Nations, as well as by many foreign dance companies. In 1994 he received the Washington, D.C., Mayor's Arts Award for Outstanding Excellence in the Arts and was an American cultural specialist for the State Department in the early 2000s. He has also taught classes worldwide. Burgess was born and raised in Santa Fe, New Mexico.

MARGARET CHO (b. 1968)

Margaret Cho is an actress and comedian born in San Francisco, California. She started performing stand-up comedy when she was only

sixteen years old and soon won a comedy contest that gave her the opportunity to open for comedian and television star Jerry Seinfeld. She eventually broke into acting, despite the lack of Asian American roles available. In 1994 she starred in her own television show, *All-American Girl*, highlighting the differences between first- and second-generation Korean Americans. After the show was canceled, Cho went on the road to perform her stand-up routine. In 1999 she created a show and eventually a movie titled *I'm the One That I Want*, which received rave reviews and many awards. Cho has also written a book and has made many television appearances, including one on *Sesame Street*. Her latest projects include her stand-up tours *Notorious C.H.O.* (2002), *Revolution* (2003), and *State of Emergency* (2004).

HERBERT Y. C. CHOY

(1916—2004) Judge Herbert Y. C. Choy was born in the little plantation town of Makaweli, on the island of Kauai. His parents, who immigrated to Hawaii as children, moved to Honolulu when Choy was five years old. Choy graduated from the University of Hawaii in 1938 and went on to study law at Harvard University, receiving his degree in 1941. He entered the U. S. Army to fight in World War II and remained on active duty until 1946, when he became a colonel in the U.S. Army Reserve. After leaving military service, he practiced law in Honolulu and served as attorney general of the Territory of Hawaii in 1957 and 1958. In May 1971, President Richard M. Nixon appointed him to the U.S. Court of Appeals, Ninth Circuit, making Judge Choy the first person of Asian ancestry to serve on the federal bench. He served until his death in 2004.

SHINAE CHUN

(b. 1943) In 2001 Shinae Chun became the highest–ranking Korean American in President George W. Bush's cabinet when she was appointed director of the Women's Bureau in the Labor Department. This department promotes equality for women in the workplace. Born to Korean parents living in Japan, Chun grew up in South Korea and studied at Ewha Women's University in Seoul. She moved to the United States in 1965 and received her master's degree in education and social policy from Northwestern University. In 1982 she helped establish the Asian American Advisory Council as a link between state government and Asian American communities. Chun also served as director of the Illinois Department of Labor from 1991 to 1999, and she authored *From the Mountains of Masan to the Land of Lincoln* and *Korean Culture—A Passage through Hermit Kingdom.*

THE CHUNG TRIO: MYUNG-WHA (b. 1944), KYUNG-WHA (b. 1948), and MYUNG-WHUN (b. 1953)

The Chung Trio are world-famous musicians who have all won top honors in international music competitions. Born in South Korea, the Chungs moved to the United States with their family in the 1960s. The trio studied music at New York's Juilliard School. The oldest, Myung-Wha Chung, is a world-renowned cellist. Sister Kyung-Wha Chung, an award-winning violinist, has played with many of the world's great orchestras. She has performed on television in both the United States and in Great Britain. Kyung-Wha has also received the South Korean Medal of Civil Merit, the highest honor bestowed by the country's government. Younger brother Myung-Whun Chung, a pianist, also plays to international audiences. In 2000 he took a position as musical director for Paris's Orchestre Philharmonique de Radio France.

KIM HYUNG-SOON (1884–1968)

Kim Hyung-Soon was a businessman who was born in Korea. He moved to the United States in 1914, where he started a small business and plant nursery in California with his friend Kim Ho. Known as the Kim Brothers Company, the business grew into an orchard and fruit-packing plant. Kim is acknowledged as the developer of several new varieties of peaches and the nectarine. Kim also helped develop the Korean American community by establishing the Korean Community Center in Los Angeles and the Korean Foundation, which gives financial aid to students of Korean ancestry.

RANDALL DUK KIM (b. 1946)

Randall Duk Kim, a Korean American actor born in Hawaii, has appeared in Broadway and off-Broadway plays. Kim began his  career playing a supporting role in a community theater production of Shakespeare's *Macbeth* and was soon portraying other Shakespearean characters in theaters throughout the United States. In 1978 Kim joined the Guthrie Theater in Minneapolis, Minnesota. Kim went on to cofound the American Players Theater in Spring Green, Wisconsin. He has also appeared on television and in films, including *The Thin Red Line* (1998), *The Replacement Killers* (1998), and *The Matrix Reloaded* (2003).

LEE CHONG-SIK (b. 1931) Dr. Lee

Chong-Sik is an important Korean American scholar. Born in Korea, Lee learned to speak Chinese and Japanese in addition to his native Korean. He moved to the United States in 1954 to study at the University of California at Los Angeles. He later received a doctorate in political science from the University of California at Berkeley. Dr. Lee taught political science at the University of Pennsylvania and coauthored an award-winning two-volume work titled *Communism in Korea* in 1973. In 2001 he published a highly praised biography of Syngman Rhee, South Korea's first president.

SAMMY LEE (b. 1920) Sammy Lee,

a second-generation Korean American born in Fresno, California, first caught the American public's attention in 1948, when he won the gold medal for high diving in the Olympic Games. Four years later, he earned the same honor, thereby becoming the first male diver in Olympic history to win the high diving medal in two consecutive Olympics. After retiring from competitive diving in 1953, Sammy Lee moved to Santa Ana, California, to coach diving and to practice medicine. In 1958 he became the first non-white athlete to receive the James E. Sullivan Award, given to the outstanding American sportsman of the year. He has also served as a member of the President's Council on Physical Fitness.

YONG-SOON MIN (b. 1953)

Artist Yong-Soon Min was born in South Korea and moved to the United States when she was seven years old. Min received bachelor's and master's degrees from the University of California at Berkeley. She works in many art mediums, including photography, drawings and paintings, and installations (groupings of objects). Min's works, many of which look at the role of women in Korea, have been shown around the world. Min also lectures, writes, and teaches at the University of California, Irvine.

ANGELA OH (b. 1955)

Angela Oh is a lawyer who first gained national attention as a spokesperson for the Korean American community after the 1992 riots in Los Angeles. Born and raised in Los Angeles, Oh attended the University of California, Davis, School of Law, where she received her law degree. She also received her master's degree in public health from the University of California, Los Angeles. Oh then practiced state and federal defense law and served as a civic leader in the Los Angeles area. After the 1992 riots, Oh was appointed as special counsel to a committee on the Los Angeles crisis. She also contributes to many prominent publications, such as the *Los Angeles Times*, *KoreAm Journal*, and various law school journals.

SANDRA OH (b. 1971)

Born in a suburb of Ottawa, Ontario, Canada, to Korean parents, Sandra Oh began acting in school plays at the age of ten. At sixteen, she was making

commercials. She went on to study acting at the National Theatre School of Canada in Montreal, Quebec, and soon began a promising career on stage and in film, winning a number of awards for her performances. Oh moved to Los Angeles in 1996 to co-star in an HBO television series, and since then she has also appeared in more than one dozen films, including the

Disney movie *The Princess Diaries* (2001), *Big Fat Liar* (2002), and *Sideways* (2004).

LINDA SUE PARK (b. 1960)

Author Linda Sue Park was born and raised in Illinois. The daughter of Korean immigrants, Park began writing when she was four years old. Her first poem was published in a children's magazine when she was only nine years old. She received a degree in English from Stanford University, near San Francisco. Park taught English as a second language, and in 1997 she decided to write her first book for children. In 1999 her first book, *Seesaw Girl*, was published. She went on to write several more books for children, and in 2002 she won the Newberry Medal (the most prestigious award for children's literature) for her book *A Single Shard*. Many of her writings are about Korea.

DR. RICHARD W. YOU

(b. 1916) Dr. Richard W. You received many national and international honors and awards in recognition of his outstanding contributions to the field of athletics and coaching. Born in Honolulu, You graduated from the University of Hawaii in 1939. He obtained his doctorate in medicine from Creighton University School of Medicine in Omaha, Nebraska, in 1943 and later became one of the two physicians selected by the U.S. Olympic Committee to accompany the U.S. Olympic team in 1952 and 1956. One of the most outstanding achievements of his career was coaching Tommy Kono, a Japanese American champion weight lifter who broke twenty-six world records and won eight world and national titles.

TIMELINE

2333 B.C.	Legendary hero Dan–Gun founds Korea.
A.D. 1392	The Chosun dynasty takes control of Korea. Confucianism becomes the driving philosophy behind government and social organization.
1637	China conquers Korea, cutting off foreign influence.
1876	Korea is forced to open its doors to the Western world for the first time in centuries.
1894	Japanese forces fight with Chinese troops for control of Korea.
1895	Japan defeats China and takes power in Korea.
1901	Drought and famine hit Korea, leaving many people starving.
1902	The first group of Korean immigrants board a boat for America.
1903	Korean immigrants to the United States arrive in Hawaii.
1905	Koreans begin moving in large numbers from the Hawaiian plantations to the U.S. mainland. Japanese rulers of Korea forbid any further Korean immigration to America.
1907	U.S. president Theodore Roosevelt agrees to a bill that forbids Asians from moving to the mainland.
1910	Japan annexes Korea, leaving Korean immigrants unable to return to their homeland. The first Korean picture brides arrive in Hawaii.

1913	California passes a law stating that only white citizens may own property.
1920	Asian immigration to the United States is further limited by the passage of the National Origins Quota Act.
1924	Immigration laws are changed, banning further Korean workers and picture brides from entering the United States.
1941	The United States enters World War II after Japan bombs Pearl Harbor, Hawaii. Korean residents support the American war effort.
1942	Japanese Americans and some Koreans are moved to relocation camps in the western United States.
1944	Congressional leaders fail to pass a bill allowing Korean immigrants to become U.S. citizens.
1945	World War II ends. The Japanese are forced to leave Korea.
1950	The Korean War breaks out between Communist forces in the northern half of Korea and U.S. and South Korean troops in the southern half.
1953	The Korean War ends. Korea remains divided into two nations, North Korea and South Korea. The second wave of Korean immigrants leave South Korea to move to the United States.
1962	Korean American Alfred Song wins a seat in the California House of Representatives, making him the first Korean American elected to the California Legislature.

1965	A new immigration bill allows Korean American medical professionals to enter the United States.
1968	Immigration laws again change, relaxing restrictions on Korean immigration.
1980	Some Korean immigrants begin remigrating to South Korea.
1992	Riots in Los Angeles destroy many Korean American businesses. Jay C. Kim is the first Korean American to be elected to Congress, representing California in the U.S. House of Representatives.
1993	Korean American Jae Soo Lim helps develop high-definition television.
1994	Chan Ho Park pitches for the Los Angeles Dodgers, the first Korean American to play major league baseball. Margaret Cho stars in her own television show, *All-American Girl*.
1999	Adult Korean American war orphans hold the first national conference of Korean adoptees.
2003	Korean Americans celebrate the one-hundred-year anniversary of the first wave of Korean immigrants to the United States.
2004	Korean Americans support the North Korea Human Rights Act. Congress passes the bill and the president signs it into law. The act allows humanitarian aid to North Koreans, as well as to North Korean defectors.

GLOSSARY

BUDDHISM: a religion that was established in India by Siddhartha Gautama (Buddha) in the fifth century B.C. Buddhism teaches that the way to enlightenment is through meditation and self-knowledge.

COMMUNISM: a political and economic system in which the government controls all industry and sets prices

CONFUCIANISM: a philosophy based on the teachings of Confucius (551—478 B.C.) that spells out civil, family, and social duties

EMIGRANT: a person who leaves his or her homeland to settle elsewhere

IMMIGRANT: a person who moves into a foreign country and settles there

KOMERICAN: a Korean American. The term is usually applied to second- or third-generation Korean Americans.

KOREATOWN: a Korean immigrant community. Koreatowns usually have their own economic and cultural foundations.

MISSIONARIES: people who work, often in a foreign land, to convert others to their religion and to carry on educational and medical work

PENINSULA: a body of land almost completely surrounded by water

PLANTATION: a large estate on which crops are grown, usually using the labor of peasant farmers or slaves

PROTECTORATE: a nation that is dependent on a stronger outside power

SOVIET UNION: a political union of fifteen republics in eastern Europe and Asia that followed Communism until the union broke up in the late twentieth century

THINGS TO SEE AND DO

BISHOP MUSEUM,
HONOLULU, HAWAII
http://www.bishopmuseum.org/
The Bishop Museum offers an
exhibit telling the story of the
Korean immigrants who arrived in
Honolulu in 1903. The exhibit covers
their hopes, their struggles, and
their successes.

CAMP MOON-HWA, ROCHESTER,
MINNESOTA
http://members.aol.com/MoonHwa/
camp.html/
Camp Moon-Hwa is an annual
weeklong culture camp for Korean
adoptees and children interested in
learning more about Korean culture
and heritage. Campers perform
traditional Korean music, wear
Korean costumes, and learn about
Korean American history.

KOREAN AMERICAN MUSEUM, LOS
ANGELES, CALIFORNIA
http://www.kamuseum.org/
Established in 1991, the Korean
American Museum (KAM) strives to
protect the heritage and history of
Korean immigrants to America.
Through its exhibitions and
programs, KAM also reaches out to

the community to recognize the
contributions of Korean immigrants
to America. The museum serves as a
bridge between generations of
Korean Americans and between
ethnic communities.

KOREAN CULTURAL SERVICE,
NEW YORK CITY
http://www.koreanculture.org/
The Korean Cultural Service was
established in 1979 to promote
understanding between Korea and
the United States. The service offers
information about Korea and
Korea–U.S. relations. It sponsors
events, exhibits, lectures, and films
to further develop strong ties
between the American and
Korean communities.

SOURCE NOTES

16   Wayne Patterson and Hyung-
      chan Kim, *Koreans in America*
      (Minneapolis: Lerner
      Publications Company, 1993), 6.

17   Lauren Lee, *Korean Americans*
      (New York: Marshall Cavendish,
      1995), 17.

21   Sa–sun Whang, quoted in
      Ronald Takaki, *From the Land of
      the Morning Calm: The Koreans in
      America* (New York: Chelsea
      House, 1994), 17.

29   Patterson and Kim, 8.

34   Sa–sun Whang, quoted in
      Takaki, 42.

40   Anna Choi, Ibid., 25.

50   Elizabeth Kim, *Ten Thousand
      Sorrows: The Extraordinary Journey
      of a Korean War Orphan* (New
      York: Doubleday, 2000), 30.

51   Sung Yong Park, quoted in
      Elaine Kim, *East to America: Korean
      American Life Stories* (New York:
      The New Press, 1996), 113.

56   Helen Zia, *Asian American
      Dreams: The Emergence of an
      American People* (New York:
      Farrar, Straus, and Giroux,
      2000), 188.

SELECTED BIBLIOGRAPHY

Encyclopedia Britannica online. N.d. http://www.britannica.com/eb/article ?eu=127867 (March 16, 2003). This on-line encyclopedia gives a complete description of the history, geography, and people of Korea, including a brief discussion of Korean immigrants.

Hyun, Peter. *Man Sei! The Making of a Korean American.* Honolulu: University of Hawaii Press, 1986. This autobiography talks about what life was like in Korea during the Japanese occupation of the early 1900s, especially before the Korean revolts of 1919. The text helps readers better understand the reasons Koreans left their homeland.

Kim, Elaine. *East to America: Korean American Life Stories.* New York: The New Press, 1996. Elaine Kim collected interviews from Korean Americans living around the United States to understand the history and complexity of the Korean community in America.

Lee, Lauren. *Korean Americans.* New York: Marshall Cavendish, 1995. Lauren Lee's book covers the Korean immigrant experience in America. Her work includes the reasons immigrants moved to the United States, the life and struggles of the early immigrants, and how Korean Americans bridge their Korean and American cultures.

Lee, Robert G. *Orientals: Asian Americans in Popular Culture.* Philadelphia: Temple University Press, 1999. This book explores the origins of the cultural stereotypes that have haunted Asian immigrants in America. Lee looks at historical events, politics, and images—both positive and negative— to uncover the Asian American experience, including that of Korean immigrants.

Nash, Amy. "Korean Americans." In *Gale Encyclopedia of Multicultural America,* edited by Jeffrey Lehman, 1071–1090. Farmington Hills, MI: Gale Group, 2000. Nash's article gives an overview of the history and reasons for Korean immigration to America. It also looks at the obstacles early immigrants faced, as well as the contributions Korean immigrants have made in American society.

Takaki, Ronald. *From the Land of the Morning Calm: The Koreans in America.* New York: Chelsea House, 1994. **This book covers the history of Korean immigration, from the first wave of immigrants escaping political and economic struggles to the most recent wave.**

"Who Are the Korean Americans?" In *The Asian American Almanac*, edited by Susan Gall, 119–129. Detroit: U.X.L., 1995. **This article covers the history** of immigration, community organizations, and the customs and traditions of Korean Americans.

Zia, Helen. *Asian American Dreams: The Emergence of an American People.* New York: Farrar, Straus, and Giroux, 2000. **Zia's work looks at the evolution of Asian Americans, including Koreans, from a relatively isolated and invisible group to a strong and influential part of American society.**

FURTHER READING & WEBSITES

NONFICTION

Behnke, Alison. *North Korea in Pictures.* Minneapolis: Lerner Publications Company, 2004. **Learn more about the culture, history, and people of North Korea.**

____. *South Korea in Pictures.* Minneapolis: Lerner Publications Company, 2004. **This book covers the history, politics, and culture of the people of South Korea.**

Feldman, Ruth Tenzer. *The Korean War.* Minneapolis: Lerner Publications Company, 2003. **Feldman examines** the events that led to Korea's division after World War II and then focuses on the North Korean invasion of South Korea in 1950.

Kim, Elizabeth. *Ten Thousand Sorrows: The Extraordinary Journey of a Korean War Orphan.* New York: Doubleday, 2000. **This biography, for older readers, follows the life of a child orphaned by the Korean War as she makes the journey from Korea to live with a family of strangers in America.**

Orr, Tamara. *The Korean Americans.* Philadelphia: Mason Crest

Publishers, 2003. Read more about the trials and tribulations of Korean immigrants who worked to build a better life in America.

Wong, Janet S. *A Suitcase of Seaweed and Other Poems.* New York: Simon & Schuster, 1996. This collection of poems by an author with Korean, Chinese, and American backgrounds describes family life and growing up as Asian American.

FICTION

Lee, Lauren. *Stella: On the Edge of Popularity.* Chicago: Polychrome Publishing, 1994. Junior high student Stella is a Korean American struggling with her American identity and her Korean heritage as she tries to fit in at her school.

Lee, Marie G. *F Is for Fabuloso.* New York: Avon Books, 1999. Korean-born Jin-Ha is quickly learning all about her new American life. Unfortunately, Jin-Ha's grades start to suffer, and she must decide whether to tell her parents or to improve her grades by studying with a tutor—one who

seems prejudiced against Korean Americans.

Na, An. *A Step from Heaven.* Asheville, NC: Front Street Press, 2001. Four-year-old Young Ju leaves Korea with her family to make a new life in the United States. The novel traces Young's life and struggles in her new home as she grows from a preschooler to a young woman.

Park, Linda Sue. *A Single Shard.* New York: Clarion Books, 2001. In this award-winning novel, a Korean war orphan sets out to take care of himself by becoming a potter in a village famous for its ware.

___. *When My Name Was Keoko.* New York: Clarion Books, 2002. In 1940 Korea, young Sun-hee struggles to maintain her heritage while living under Japanese oppression.

WEBSITES

ASIANINFO.ORG
http://www.asianinfo.org/asianinfo/korea/about_korea.htm
This website has links to the arts, literature, social customs,

businesses, and history of several Asian countries, including Korea. It also features links to newspapers and government organizations, as well as country profiles.

INAMERICABOOKS.COM

http://www.inamericabooks.com

Visit inamericabooks.com, the on-line home of the In America series, to get linked to all sorts of useful information. You'll find historical and cultural websites related to individual groups, as well as general information on genealogy, creating your own family tree, and the history of immigration in America.

KOREAN CULTURAL CENTER

http://www.kccla.org

The website for the Korean Cultural Center features information about the center's exhibits, festivals, and lectures. The center also houses a seventeen-thousand-volume library with an online catalog and a museum that offers a virtual tour.

KOREAWEB

http://koreaweb.ws/9_koream.html

This site offers links to Korean American organizations, communities, and more.

NATIONAL ASSOCIATION OF KOREAN AMERICANS (NAKA)

http://www.naka.org

Founded in 1994, this organization works to improve civil rights for Korean Americans. NAKA's website includes news that affects Korean Americans, as well as links to resources and other programs.

INDEX

web enhanced at **www.inamericabooks.com**

ACKNOWLEDGMENTS: THE PHOTOGRAPHS IN THIS BOOK ARE REPRODUCED WITH THE PERMISSION OF: Digital Vision Royalty Free, pp. 3, 20; © TRIP/TRIP, p. 6; Bill Hauser, pp. 7, 37; © TRIP/R. Nichols, p. 10; California Academy of Sciences, p. 11; Library of Congress, pp. 13 (LC–USZ62–72798), 15 (LC–USZ62–72614), 16 (LC–USZ62–108293), 19 (LC–USZ62–72622), 21, 36 (LC–USZC4–11867); Bishop Museum, pp. 22, 23, 25, 26, 30, 38; Shades of L.A. Archives/Los Angeles Public Library, pp. 28, 35, 41, 43, 46; R. J. Baker, Bishop Museum, p. 33; USIA, p. 49 (Photo No. 306–PS–51–16809);   Herald Examiner Collection/Los Angeles Public Library, p. 53; © TRIP/M. Barlow, p. 54; © Peter Turnley/CORBIS, p. 55; © Richard B. Levine , p. 57; Library of Congress (LC–USZC4–6060), courtesy Yong Soon Min, 1990, p. 59; AP/Wide World Photos, p. 60; © Tommy and Ji Choi, p. 61 (both); Photo courtesy Mary Noble Ours/Dana Tai Soon Burgess, p. 62 (left); © Pat Thompson/Zuma Press, p. 62 (right); U.S. Courts for the Ninth Circuit , p. 63; © Paul Mounce/CORBIS, p. 64; © EMPICS/Zuma Press, p. 65; Photo courtesy Yong Soon Min, p. 66 (left); © Lisa O'Connor/Zuma Press, p. 66 (right); © Klaus Pollmeier, p. 67.

Front Cover: Digital Vision Royalty Free (title); © Richard B. Levine (center); © TRIP/TRIP (bottom). Back Cover: Digital Vision Royalty Free.